MADE FROM A TREE

BY ROBERT R. O'BRIEN

Harcourt

Orlando   Boston   Dallas   Chicago   San Diego

Visit *The Learning Site!*

www.harcourtschool.com

Trees are beautiful. They are also useful. Trees are used to make many things. Can you think of something that is made from a tree?

Trees are used for firewood. People burn the wood in fireplaces and stoves. The wood keeps families warm in the winter.

Trees are used for paper. Wood
gets ground up into little pieces.
The pieces get mixed into a paste.

The paste gets rolled out. It is
pressed into long sheets. The
sheets get cut up to make paper.

Trees are used for lumber. Lumber
is used to build houses. Lumber
can also be used to make things
like fences and shelves.

Trees are used for making boats.
Canoes and boats are made
from wood.

Trees are used for toys. This Russian doll is carved out of wood. Each piece opens up to hold another doll.

Trees are used for making musical instruments. Violins are made from wood. Guitars are made from wood. Many drums are made from wood.

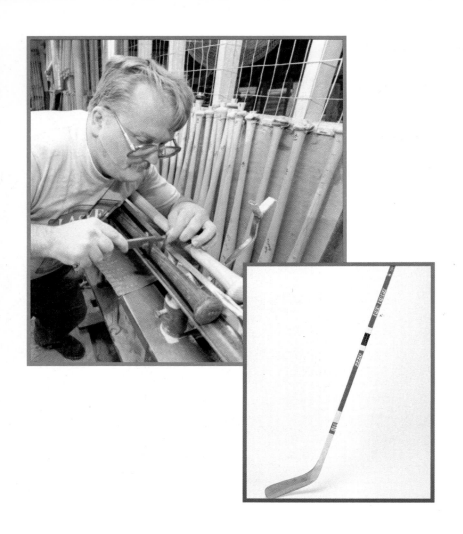

Trees are used to make sports
equipment. Baseball bats are made
from wood. Hockey sticks and
lacrosse sticks are made from wood.

Trees are used for making school
supplies. Pencils are made from
wood. Paper is made from wood.
Rulers are made from wood.

Trees are used for playgrounds.
Many playground gyms are made
from wood. Slides and benches can
be made from wood.

Trees are used for making long, tall things. Flagpoles, telephone poles, and totem poles are made from trees.

Trees are used for making small things. Toothpicks, matchsticks, and beads can all be made from wood.

Trees are used to make furniture.
We sit on chairs made of wood.
We sleep on beds made of wood.
We eat on tables made of wood.

Trees can be used to make things
we use every day. Look around.
Everywhere you look, you can
see something made from a tree.